Aphorisms and Comments

Aphorisms and Comments

on Nassim Nicholas Taleb's *Incerto*

Maximilian Hirner

Dedicated to Nassim Nicholas Taleb, my
Mentor and Teacher, who is worthy to be
called Father.

Contact

©Maximilian Hirner, 2019

- Mail: a.u.k.nnt@gmail.com

- Facebook (English): https://www.facebook.com/
  Aphorisms.and.Comments.Incerto/

- Facebook (German): https://www.facebook.com/
  Aphorismen.und.Kommentare.Incerto/

- Twitter: @Maximilian_H1

- medium.com: @Maximilian_H1

If you think that my works are worth it, feel free to make a gift here:

- paypal.me/MaximilianH1

Special Thanks to:

My test-readers Dominic V. C. Parker, Dr. Stefan A. Roth, Michael Lackner, and Schulbert Koleka

The truly great scholars (you know who you are) whom I was allowed to ask questions and make suggestions to despite neither having a PhD nor a million $$ in my account

Nicholas Teague and Prof. Yaneer Bar-Yam for further Inspirations

The "Incerto" discussion group on Fb

Dennis Häggblom who proved to me that I'm not hubristic for following Maestro Taleb, writing an aphorism book

And of course to Maestro Taleb, who catalysed my thoughts.

Furthermore Thanks to:

My brother Frdß

My co-managers of the FabLab, where I spent many days (and nights) for work

My old colleagues Martin and Christian, for many discussions over coffee

The "Capt'n" from Munich, who's maybe less crazy than many other people out there

Foreword

The inspiration(s) for this book came from the best aphorists of world history: Lichtenberg, Montaigne, Goethe, Nietzsche, Karl Kraus, and of course Nassim Nicholas Taleb.

If you want to dig deeper into Taleb's concepts, I hope these comments may help you a bit with it.

What I did isn't much – I just applied his concepts to the world and the thoughts other people had about it (and said thoughts), but still managed to come to some interesting conclusions, and have some ideas of my own.

Since I am too lazy to do more work, I decided to write a book of aphorisms, delivering as much information to you as possible in a text as short as possible. In 2014, I discovered Taleb's books (starting with "Antifragile"); in 2016, I contacted him via the social networks; in 2018, I decided to write my first book, inspired by him.

Maestro Taleb is with little doubt the greatest living philosopher and polymath. He changed my way of thinking, and catalysed it. For all I learned from him, I owe him a lot. This book shall pay off some of this intellectual debt, among other tings.
12

That's it.

Glossary

I have thought back and forth whether to include a glossary in this book or not. The aphorisms should be able to speak for themselves. But it certainly won't hurt if I express some of Maestro Taleb's terms in my own words.

- **Black Swans**: Very real events which for some reasons nobody managed to predict. Often catastrophic, but sometimes positive developments – e. g. the Internet.

- **Fat Tony**: An *Incerto* character. An Italian-American from the NY metropolitan area who became a multi-millionaire at the stock market. Totally uneducated an unerudite (not like N. N. Taleb), but knows one ting very well: There are fools. And that's the reason he became rich (and fat).

- **Iatrogenics**: Health problems caused by the healer.

- **Lindy Effect**: Many things and concepts (other than living beings) will survive for longer if they have existed for longer. A building that has existed for millennia (like the Pyramids) will probably continue to exist for millennia.

- *via negativa*: The way to solve your problems by cutting out things. If you have health problems, you could e. g. quit smoking or avoid certain kinds of food. Opposite of the *via positiva*, where you think that your problems are caused by the fact that you are missing something.

Contents

Aphorisms

- Jesus understood Mediocristan and Extremistan, although these words weren't part of his vocabulary. "But other fell into good ground, and brought forth fruit, some an hundredfold, some sixtyfold, some thirtyfold."

Contents

Chapter 1

Maestro Taleb

1. Along the lines of Maestro Taleb's antifragility: What's the anti-chain? What *won't* fail as soon as the weakest link will be broken? What's redundant by nature?

* * *

2. Maestro Taleb's thought "...and idiots [think] in labels" might be his deepest.

* * *

3. Maestro Taleb goes the hard way of virtue, like Hercules.

* * *

4. Maestro Taleb grew up in Amioun, but became rich and famous in New York. Which place is more important for him?

* * *

5. When Maestro Taleb says that theater works best when actors wear masks, he is thinking like a true Greek.

* * *

6. Left or right: If one kind of people reads & understands Maestro Taleb, and the other kind doesn't, then the latter have a problem.

* * *

7. Antaios and earth... some people interpret this as "soil"
   – Maestro Taleb explains it's rather "reality". And he
   nailed it.

* * *

8. Maestro Taleb isn't just good in trading, statistics, dead-
   lifting, history, and linguistics, but making enemies too.

* * *

9. Please Maestro, leave some unsolved big questions for
   the younger people.

* * *

10. Maestro, you're a true Greek... better being hit by
    Tyche's arrow than reading bad news from all over the
    world and worry.

* * *

11. What should we do if lawyers or judges fragilize the world, Maestro?

* * *

12. Fat Tony would just laugh about the fact that intelligent people spend time thinking about Newcomb's Paradoxon.

* * *

13. What would Fat Tony do, if the rest of the world told him that 2+2=5?

* * *

14. The Roman emperors were the Fat Tonys of their time.

* * *

15. Maestro Taleb says: "When people call you intelligent it is almost always because they agree with you. Other-

wise, they would call you arrogant." The bigger problem
are the people who call you (or me, or anyone) intelligent even if you're wrong, just because they agree with
you.

* * *

16. Maestro, if you can forget the words and deeds of the
fools, you're truly enviable.

* * *

17. If you are arrogant, you should be really smart as well.
Maestro Taleb is this, as one among few.

24

Chapter 2

Maestro Taleb's concepts

1. The human character is definitely from Extremistan. That's why both Jesus and Hitler were possible. And even if you know 10000 people in person...

* * *

2. About the Theseus Paradoxon: Small changes are from Mediocristan, big ones from Extremistan!

* * *

3. Ignorance is fragile.

* * *

4. Lies are fragile... they demand more effort, others can refute them, you can fail because of them.

* * *

5. If the Lindy Effect is true, in times of crisis the older Entities should rather survive.

* * *

6. What's the equivalent of Iatrogenics, but for lawyers?

* * *

7. If the Big is platonic, one has to learn that small=beautiful.

* * *

8. Because of the growing Isolation of the people, we are
getting deeper into Extremistan too.

* * *

9. It's not the concentration of capital that matters, but
only Asymmetry. The latter creates the concentration!

* * *

10. Cicero removed corrupt Politicians like Catalina by *via
negativa* out of Roman politics, in his job as a lawyer.

* * *

11. Intellectuals are anti-smart.

* * *

12. Life in Extremistan: Great hopes, even bigger disap-
pointments.

* * *

13. How do you avoid unfair asymmetries, if the world is so heterogenous?

* * *

14. Extremistan is seductive... but people always overestimate their chance to rise to the top.

* * *

15. Naivety is fragile.

* * *

16. From the Unknown, not to say Unprovable, come the Black Swans.

* * *

17. John Wilkins' beautifully ordered language is the very
opposite of redundant – hence, we should expect it to
be very fragile too.

* * *

18. Programmers work in Extremistan too.

* * *

19. The Green Revolution was a Black Swan too.

* * *

20. Some people owe us money for the Anti-knowledge they
spread.

* * *

21. I had left academia some months ago when discovering "Antifragile". Seeing there was this smart guy with fuck-you money who told me I had done the right choice...

* * *

22. Yeah, that'd be some civilization that invented social science before the mahket.

* * *

23. What's robust/Antifragile in one aspect might be fragile in a different one.

* * *

24. If the Lindy effect applies to democracies, that'd be good news for democracies. – And what about other political systems?

* * *

25. Machines are from Mediocristan, humans from Extremistan?

* * *

26. Apropos "They would try to eliminate seasons" – there
are places in the world w/o seasons. They're called
deserts.

* * *

27. Whose fault is it, when the Fire will break out? The
fool who made the first spark – or the fools who poured
out gasoline everywhere?

* * *

28. Fat incomes for the "rent-seekers" as the dole for those
poor in spirit.

* * *

29. Hard to follow *via negativa* if some people only know one ting.

* * *

30. What's the appropriate thing to do with fragilising parents?

* * *

31. Stoics should be immune against insults, but also against gushing praise. What's more important in practice?

* * *

32. That which the common people are doing tends to be more Lindy, since they have literally more experience with it.

* * *

33. Maybe we have to describe the meaning of life in a negative way too.

Chapter 3

Religion

1. If really everything in this world will pass away one day, it explains why people wish for something eternal.

* * *

2. Jesus said things in a language every child could understand. He did not show off with supposed magic formulas like a charlatan.

* * *

3. For the Romans, Yahweh was a Black Swan.

* * *

4. The ancient Germanic religion was as fragile as their holy oaks, unfortunately for them.

* * *

5. The Jews have seen many bodies of their enemies float down the river.

* * *

6. Sloth might be a mortal sin, but it's not mentioned in the Ten Commandments.

* * *

7. In old times, only the most privileged were able to spend time thinking about religion. Today, only the least privileged (unemployed, prisoners) can do so – anyone else is too busy.

$$* \quad * \quad *$$

8. If we managed to find out what lead to the End of the Golden Age of Islam, at least people there would not have suffered for nothing.

$$* \quad * \quad *$$

9. Nothing in the Ten Commandments mentions that you aren't allowed to call a fool a fool.

$$* \quad * \quad *$$

10. Drone pilots don't risk their Life, but their Soul, if they have one.

$$* \quad * \quad *$$

11. Sometimes I think: God would be easier to explain than the soul.

$$* \quad * \quad *$$

12. How would religious people explain God's Creation to their kids in the future, *if there wasn't any left?*

* * *

13. Prophets have told their followers to fast, give money, fight for their religion, even die... but slow poisoning?

* * *

14. Religions are supposed to be eternal truths. Makes a bad impression if you change them for no good reason.

* * *

15. This kind of gushing annoys me too, esp. comparisons to gods. – As long as they can't walk on water, they aren't gods to me.

* * *

16. Why should I pray to an AI?

* * *

17. Maybe we should start to talk about "atheists" and "apracticists" as well, which are two different things, obviously?

Chapter 4

Other famous people

1. Kahneman & Tversky write about an economist in the US who will buy a bottle of wine only if he's got to pay less than 10$, and only sells it if he gets more than 30$ for it. If all people thought like that, there'd be very little trade in the world.

* * *

2. At first came Goethe, then his imitators, who got in the way for the public... and because of their flaws it was their fault when people started to dislike even Goethe. – Only after these imitators had wilted, died, and been forgotten, Goethe became clearly visible again.

* * *

3. Alexander the Great actually punished the Spartans when he refrained from conquering them.

* * *

4. Yes, Ricardo has limits.

* * *

5. Trotsky reached the final table, but Stalin won the poker tournament for power.

* * *

6. Yes, Ayn Rand, Grey is a mixture of Black and White.

* * *

7. Andy Warhol's 15 Minutes rather probably mean that
there'll be just 15 minutes time of fame left per artist,
since there are so many of them. So much about fame
for eternity.

* * *

8. Newton had an excuse. Gravity is a two-body problem,
the stock market a thousand-spirits problem.

* * *

9. Umberto Eco went to school under fascism, had to write
how he even prayed for the Duce, but was aware all the
time it wasn't true. Indoctrination doesn't work as well
as some people think.

* * *

10. The leftists don't like Spengler, because he's a rightist;
and the German rightists don't, because they've had
enough of downfalls since 1945.

** * **

11. Who's more wrong? Pinker – or some historicist who claims that a big war is coming?

** * **

12. People don't like people who win by not doing something. Like Quintus Fabius Cunctator.

Chapter 5

Politics

1. Stress accelerates your heartbeat, thus shortening life. By this way, ISIS/AQ have killed many more people.

* * *

2. Is it easier to destroy borders or to build them?

* * *

3. The modern Bureaucratic state is like a Brontosaurus: Harmless for little agile carnivores, but probably tramples those it is supposed to protect to death. Only impressive at the first glance.

* * *

4. The Problem with racism: It is too easy.

* * *

5. Don't expect too much from becoming a tyrant.

* * *

6. Only the three C's are willing to work under a Tyrant: Crazies, Criminals, and Captives.

* * *

7. So many ideologies... and their adherents are so busy
   reading and discussing the available books, they don't
   have any time left for anything else.

* * *

8. Being a member in two political parties, at the same
   time... isn't that as if you were both defendant and
   plaintiff in court? Or at least defendant and witness?

* * *

9. Typical politicians are just good enough to pretend
   to 50% of the people that they'd understand anything
   about governing.

* * *

10. We tawk so much about forms of government and con-
    stitutions, but so much more depends on scaling, re-
    garding the population that has grown.

* * *

11. If someone has a piece of the power, someone else can-
    not have the same piece of power.

* * *

12. No politician of today resigns because he's too old, too
    dumb, or too bad.

* * *

13. Are there religious people who want to understand cap-
    italism?

* * *

14. German Libertarians? Seems to me like American Com-
    munists. They exist, but it makes no sense.

* * *

15. One day, children will ask: "Why didn't anyone say
    anything?" And the answer will have to be: "Some peo-

ple did say something. But our elites were conceited fools."

* * *

16. Anyone who deems spin-doctoring and empty promises more important than real achievements by somewhat grumpy people, shall try to eat his empty promises.

* * *

17. A tyrant who has all intelligent people killed who find a fault, and all brave people who speak against him despite of threats, will only reign cowards and fools at the end.

* * *

18. The problem isn't after all that the nazis would just have trolled the Jews and Leftists a bit.

* * *

19. It is as if Greece, the Lebanon etc. were a mixture of the Hanse cities and Switzerland. Plus olive oil and sun.

* * *

20. Politicians have felt insulted for decades, whenever they're for a few seconds less on TV than their opponents... none of them ever gets that people might have enough of them.

* * *

21. There'd be less shouting if the leftists had to pay with their own money for refugees – and the rightists had to risk their lives shooting on Islamists.

* * *

22. Ideology rhymes with idiocy. No coincidence.

* * *

23. Politicians thinking too highly of themselves is probably
the biggest problem today.

* * *

24. Many occupations are in a crisis of Legitimacy today...
party politicians most of all.

* * *

25. Today, both sides claim the other one was in denial.
They only differ about the object: Global Warming or
radical Islamism?

* * *

26. An intelligent conservative holds on to what will stay;
a dumb one holds on to what is doomed to fall.

* * *

27. A rulership of those people who think truly long-term – there is no word yet for this.

* * *

28. To the neonazis and other neo-X: Repetitions don't please!

* * *

29. The problem if you're the guy who dares to say everything: People can imagine you saying everything.

* * *

30. Power vacua are rare, competence vacua common.

* * *

31. Nothing can end well, if people have to be loyal to a fool or fraudster.

Chapter 6

Science and education

1. The damaged education system of today will lead to a lot of Anti-Intellectualism in the future.

* * *

2. I love reading, thinking, and science, thus hate the academic system.

* * *

3. Writing the history of the great refutations.

* * *

4. Sometimes people learn the words before the things, but mostly the other way round.

* * *

5. When they read only third and fourth derivates at the universities, any amateur who reads and understands the Originals will be their superior.

* * *

6. Many students have to sit around in school like pensioners who don't know what to do in retirement.

* * *

7. Typical exams in school count the mistakes, not the especially positive achievements!

* * *

8. One day, the helicopter moms won't be there anymore to protect their kids from everything. And then they'll be facing the world, with a Practice Quotient below room temperature.

* * *

9. When people have to estimate the height of the Empire State Building (swarm intelligence), there's neither fear nor greed involved.

* * *

10. Impressionist knowledge.

* * *

11. It is hard to tell whether the modern education system improved the IQ. But it certainly reduced the Practice Quotient.

* * *

12. The kids from the ghettos at least immediately know that their schools are garbage. The white middle class kids won't notice that quickly.

* * *

13. If scientists aren't speaking about truth, other people who know less will still do.

* * *

14. The four things a good scientist needs: Curiosity, scepticism, logic, statistics.

* * *

15. The physicists have it easier, in a certain sense. Electrons don't envy each other and also don't ape each other.

* * *

16. The knowledge of Mankind grows, but every single human is still born an ignorant.

$$* * *$$

17. You learn from mistakes? Then it's even worse that some people never want to admit their mistakes.

$$* * *$$

18. As long as the people are able to learn, fake news cannot hurt them.

Chapter 7

Arts

1. A truly great author should be able to write a great book if he lived in the Brave New World and didn't know any language but Newspeak.

* * *

2. A great storyteller descends to Hell to grill steaks, visits God afterwards for tea, and tells us the tale about everything.

* * *

3. A *great* artist has both feet on the ground and still has the head in the clouds at the same time.

* * *

4. The second-best thing an author can do for his fans is delivering a new work that fulfills 100% of their expectations. The best would be if he delivers a new work that fulfills none of their expectations but is still loved by them.

* * *

5. The act of drawing probably is an even bigger artwork than the finished drawing.

* * *

6. It'd have to be a punishment for a true music lover if he was swamped with great music until he can't hear it anymore.

* * *

7. At the end of Wagner's "Ring" the heroes lose, instead
of building an empire lasting a thousand years.

* * *

8. People spend less time in a forest or with a good book
than they spend in the bathroom. It's not surprising
they have too much excrement in their heads.

* * *

9. Many artists were born in the countryside or small
cities, but became famous in the capital. What's more
important for culture now?

* * *

10. Fantasy is related to the ability to remember the past
and to plan the future.

Chapter 8

Money, Markets, etc.

1. amazon proves: Chaos *is* better organised.

* * *

2. What do the critics of compounded interest say about the so-called zero / minus interest?

* * *

3. The temporary employment dissolved the workforce.

* * *

4. If you create material incentives, the idealists in this area will be "swamped".

* * *

5. The supposed "secret" of compound interest? Most people can only think in a linear way, not exponentially!

* * *

6. What's the easiest way to have wealth for everyone? – If it's naturally there.

* * *

7. Anyone who believes that, is right most of the time – just like the people who think that stocks on the market could go up exclusively.

* * *

8. Why did people even forget crop rotation with the down-
fall of the Roman Empire? Field work was done by
slaves, and the free people weren't interested in how
that work was done. This whole situation was "good
enough".

* * *

9. If the world will become *even more* oligarchic in the
future, it'll become more volatile and illiquid as well.

* * *

10. The fascinating thing about money is the potential.
Spend it, and you have a certain amount of houses,
cars, gold or diamonds. Keep it, and you have *the Op-
tion* for all that and more. Spend it, and these options
are gone.

* * *

11. If inequality grows, the rich profit more, but what are
we supposed to do? All of this did not happen because
someone pushed a big lever towards "inequality".

* * *

12. If debtors = slaves, will we see uprisings of debtors in the future, like with Spartacus in Rome?

Chapter 9

Truth

1. I want to tear open the soil of thoughts and plough it up, and while I'm at this, I too often find boiling Lava, because I go that deep. But volcanic soil is the most fertile, and volcanic stone the hardest.

* * *

2. In the material world, there are no paradoxa like those caused by categories in the mental world. An atom can't be a true part of itself. There just is no non-trivial self-reference.

* * *

3. Some sentences contain a lot of Information, some are just full of hot air. How to tell them apart?

* * *

4. Sometimes, reality is complex. Sometimes, everything is made more complicated on purpose.

* * *

5. Sometimes every single sentence is as clear as crystal, but taken together, they become an enigma.

* * *

6. At the beginning, constraints are a support, but when they stay and multiply, at the end they'll block everything.

* * *

7. We don't live in the age of truth and lies anymore, but
in the age of bullshit? ...

* * *

8. The easiest ideas are sometimes hardest to find.

* * *

9. There's only one truth, but an infinity of lies.

* * *

10. Lies and crimes mean challenging truth itself.

* * *

11. Nothing is greater, more beautiful and yet more horrific
than truth.

* * *

12. The parable of the six blind men and the elephant shows
    us that truth can have many sides. But it also says
    implicitly that many things may exist which aren't the
    least like an elephant.

Chapter 10

Societies

1. Simply everything goes faster in cities. But carrying babies to full term still takes nine months.

* * *

2. Humans don't act anymore like *homo sapiens sapiens* who can think, but like Robots in beaten tracks. If anything doesn't work according to plan, their whole System crashes. It is truly a shame if people don't want to think.

* * *

3. The bigger a society, the more fractal it is...

* * *

4. The more people there are, the faster we have to run, to be the first one who finds the solution for a problem. Hence, we get faster and faster into a mellowed situation. The world gets more boring.

* * *

5. The bigger an entity, the more people are just underlings.

* * *

6. The division of modern society also divides responsibility in an unclear way.

* * *

7. There are more old people around than ever in world
history – but not a bit more wisdom.

* * *

8. The whole damn world is a commons!

* * *

9. The best way to keep distance from an evil: Living in a
society where it's unknown yet – or forgotten already.

* * *

10. Never to be the slave of bad people.

* * *

11. An older human should not brag how the youth didn't
witness the time he lived through. He also did not
witness most of world history.

* * *

12. A fool who collects lots of data is a fool with lots of data.

* * *

13. Germany. A difficult country with a difficult people.

* * *

14. Today, people are able to consume news about crimes and catastrophes of the whole world... but even for a great Man, that'd become too much at the end of the day.

* * *

15. When people are afraid, they tend to follow the letter of the law.

* * *

16. Every development is good for someone. That doesn't
mean that the profiteers have worked 24/7 for it when
it happens.

* * *

17. It says a lot about the crisis of journalism that three of
the most important people who did investigative work
today weren't journalists: Manning was an IT special-
ist, Snowden as well, Assange...

* * *

18. The journalists might be the perception organs of society, but they aren't the brain. Sometimes you have to
ask yourself whether you can still trust your own eyes.

* * *

19. When everyone's corruptible, someone who's guaran-
teed to be incorruptible would be a huge danger.

* * *

20. When you use a certain new weapon, your opponent may too.

* * *

21. It makes sense to have different rules for guns in New York or an Appalachian village.

* * *

22. Probably "making better use of resources / discovering new ones" should have priority #1.

* * *

23. Murderers on death row get a last meal, risk takers maybe not even that.

* * *

24. A society made up of zeroes cannot last.

* * *

25. If a human is unable to do his task, he'll be even more unable to choose a better successor.

Chapter 11

Thoughts

1. The inseparability of the human in practice.

* * *

2. Objects in the future, once noticed, look closer than they really are.

* * *

3. It doesn't matter that much to have a bulletproof plan, but rather training how to make plans.

* * *

4. Where I flee to, anyone else might come to as well.

* * *

5. If the being of the humans can't be changed – can we at least tell which part of the human being is the problem, then?

* * *

6. *Tone* of color.

* * *

7. Thought control only hits people who are still able and willing to think.

* * *

8. Could "rolled up" dimensions of time exist?

* * *

9. An explanation can be great, but it doesn't have to be
a consolation because of that.

* * *

10. Middle class – Middle man – Middle way – Mediator –
Mediocre – Meddling

* * *

11. If you dumb down your message so much that even the
biggest fool can understand it, only the biggest fool will
follow you.

* * *

12. If we only "construct" the perceived world, why don't people think up something better? Like a world without pederasts, terrorists and chemical weapons?

* * *

13. I don't believe we live in a simulation. Just consider how hard it'd be to simulate some billion helium atoms in a box, let alone our whole world.

* * *

14. How do you do training for youth?

* * *

15. The words "awesome", "fantastic" and even "divine" are used way too often nowadays for totally mundane stuff.

* * *

16. Because no one can be omniscient, and the world changes,
    you need people who have new ideas. For this reason
    alone, we should tolerate people who think differently.
    Everyone can find his place by this way: process starters
    and brakesmen, the determined and the hesitant ones,
    the conformists and the revolutionaries, the partisans
    and those who change sides, those who give 150% and
    the halfhearted, the serious ones and the mockers.

Chapter 12

Moral

1. It'd be horrible to sacrifice many human lives to realize a specific purpose. But it'd be even more horrible to sacrifice many human lives for no purpose at all.

$$* * *$$

2. Yes, one can be a bad person, even when one never murders, never steals, never cheats and never (consciously) lies.

$$* * *$$

3. Is there such a thing as Post-cynicism?

* * *

4. Yes, this is the biggest tension anywhere: The wish to be successful and morally good at the same time.

* * *

5. How evil has its place: As a warning that humans are able to do it; to remember us to defend against it; so some can go the way of evil and fail in a demonstrative way; and to train for a fight against a bigger evil.

* * *

6. The opposite of good parents aren't the childless. It's those "parents" who wouldn't care if their own children perished.

Chapter 13

Misc.

1. It's been "a minute to twelve" many times already, but
   time still passes and has no mercy.

* * *

2. That's the biggest fight against oneself: Admitting that
   one might be wrong.

* * *

3. What most people remember of a two-hour talk generally can be subsumed in five minutes. Hence, you could say it in five minutes from the beginning.

* * *

4. We often stumble blindly through the Darkness (or fog) – but sometimes, that's the way we stumble over the big treasure.

* * *

5. If you have a stone bound around your neck, and the water is rising above your head: Cut the rope, or drown!

* * *

6. On the one hand, the problems are bigger than ever, on the other hand, people are prepared worse for them than ever.

* * *

7. The rainforest gets destroyed, many species are eradicated, infrastructure and education decay, but may God prevent that some fool gets insulted.

* * *

8. How do you tell someone diplomatically that he is a fool and caused the problem?

* * *

9. At the end of the day, we don't want after all that people only fill out forms in the correct way.

* * *

10. Of all the post-somethings, I dislike few as much as the very concept of postmeritocracy.

* * *

11. It's easier to destroy than building up – which seems to include borders.

* * *

12. Everyone is throwing dirt nowadays... not a single problem is solved, there's just more dirt in the world and in the heads.

* * *

13. Life always means survival – thus, "be fruitful and multiply" is a very dangerous heuristic if there's already overpopulation.

* * *

14. We don't want a dead order like on a chess board, but also no chaos like a garbage dump.

* * *

15. You can get bad results even if you use good tools.

Chapter 14

Finally...

- Nobody ever said "Stulta lex sed lex"!

"Max is good!" – Nassim Nicholas Taleb, Real World Risk Seminar, Feb. 2017

"You've got a sharp mind!" – Yaneer Bar-Yam

"Maximilian Hirner, you must be a genius." – Marsden Katana

"A praise from NNT or YBY is worth more than the best review from the NYT." – Maximilian Hirner

www.ingramcontent.com/pod-product-compliance
Lightning Source LLC
Chambersburg PA
CBHW051213250726
48655CB00006B/2385